KEYBOARD PERCUSSION

CONCERT FAVORITES

Volume 2

Band Arrangements Correlated with
Essential Elements Band Method Book 1

ISBN 978-1-4234-0089-9

HAL•LEONARD®

7777 W. BLUEMOUND RD. P.O. BOX 13819 MILWAUKEE, WI 53213

00860177

BANDROOM BOOGIE

KEYBOARD PERCUSSION
Bells

MICHAEL SWEENEY

BEETHOVEN'S NINTH

KEYBOARD PERCUSSION
(Bells)

LUDWIG VAN BEETHOVEN
Arranged by PAUL LAVENDER

GALLANT MARCH

KEYBOARD PERCUSSION
Bells

MICHAEL SWEENEY

HIGH ADVENTURE

KEYBOARD PERCUSSION
Bells

PAUL LAVENDER

ROCK & ROLL - PART II
(The Hey Song)

KEYBOARD PERCUSSION
Bells

Words and Music by
MIKE LEANDER and GARY GLITTER
Arranged by PAUL LAVENDER

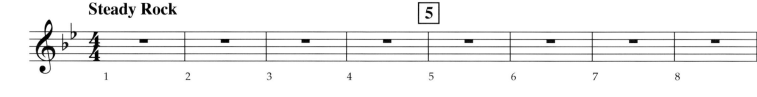

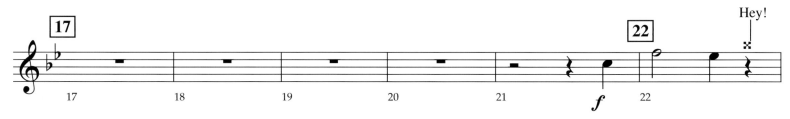

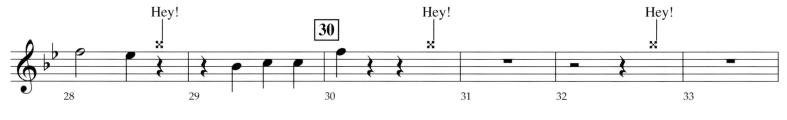

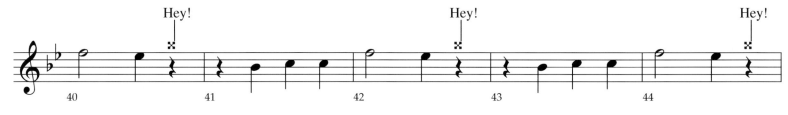

00860177

AMAZING GRACE

KEYBOARD PERCUSSION
Bells

Traditional American Melody
Arranged by PAUL LAVENDER

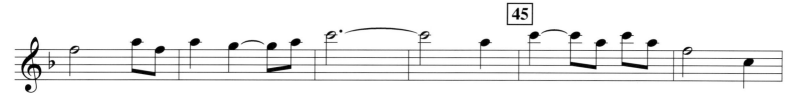

KEYBOARD PERCUSSION
(Bells)

INFINITY
(Concert March)

JAMES CURNOW (ASCAP)

LATIN FIRE

KEYBOARD PERCUSSION
Bells

JOHN HIGGINS

00860177

LINUS AND LUCY

KEYBOARD PERCUSSION
Bells

By VINCE GUARALDI
Arranged by MICHAEL SWEENEY

00860177

THEME FROM "STAR TREK® GENERATIONS" 11

KEYBOARD PERCUSSION
(Bells)

Music by DENNIS McCARTHY
Arranged by MICHAEL SWEENEY

AMERICAN SPIRIT MARCH

KEYBOARD PERCUSSION
Bells

JOHN HIGGINS

GATHERING IN THE GLEN

KEYBOARD PERCUSSION
Bells

MICHAEL SWEENEY

00860177

THE LOCO-MOTION

KEYBOARD PERCUSSION
Bells

Words and Music by
GERRY GOFFIN and CAROLE KING
Arranged by JOHN HIGGINS

00860177

ROYAL FIREWORKS MUSIC

KEYBOARD PERCUSSION
Bells

GEORGE FREDERIC HANDEL
Arranged by MICHAEL SWEENEY

0860177

SCARBOROUGH FAIR

KEYBOARD PERCUSSION
Bells

Traditional English
Arranged by JOHN MOSS

Cantabile Moderato